MICHAEL DAUGHERTY

STRUT

FOR STRING ORCHESTRA
(1989)

HENDON MUSIC

BOOSEY & HAWKES

AN IMAGEM COMPANY

DISTRIBUTED BY

HAL•LEONARD®
CORPORATION
7777 W. BLUEMOUND RD. P.O. BOX 13819 MILWAUKEE, WI 53213

www.boosey.com
www.halleonard.com

Published by Hendon Music, Inc.
a Boosey & Hawkes company
229 West 28th Street, 11th Floor
New York NY 10001

www.boosey.com

ISMN 979-0-051-09682-4

Cover image: Winold Reiss, *Interpretation of Harlem* (1920); Public Domain
Photography: Paul Robeson in Eugene O'Neill's *The Emperor Jones* (1933); Public Domain
Music Engraving by Stephen Nolan

Commissioned by New York State School Music Association

First performed by New York All-State String Orchestra
conducted by Larry Rachleff
at the 1989 NYSSMA Conference
on October 15, 1989

First recorded by the Miramar Sinfonietta
conducted by Henri B. Pensis
on *Twentieth Century Contrasts*
Albany Music 509

Performance materials are available from the Boosey & Hawkes Rental Library
www.boosey.com

BIOGRAPHY

Grammy® Award winning composer Michael Daugherty is one of the most commissioned, performed, and recorded composers on the American concert music scene today. His music is rich with cultural allusions and bears the stamp of classic modernism, with colliding tonalities and blocks of sound; at the same time, his melodies can be eloquent and stirring. Daugherty has been hailed by *The Times* (London) as "a master icon maker" with a "maverick imagination, fearless structural sense and meticulous ear."

Daugherty first came to international attention when the Baltimore Symphony Orchestra, conducted by David Zinman, performed his *Metropolis Symphony* at Carnegie Hall in 1994. Since that time, Daugherty's music has entered the orchestral, band and chamber music repertory and made him, according to the League of American Orchestras, one of the ten most performed American composers. In 2011, the Nashville Symphony's Naxos recording of Daugherty's *Metropolis Symphony* and *Deus ex Machina* was honored with three Grammy® Awards, including Best Classical Contemporary Composition.

Born in 1954 in Cedar Rapids, Iowa, Daugherty is the son of a dance-band drummer and the oldest of five brothers, all professional musicians. He studied music composition at the University of North Texas (1972-76), the Manhattan School of Music (1976-78), and computer music at Pierre Boulez's IRCAM in Paris (1979-80). Daugherty received his doctorate from Yale University in 1986 where his teachers included Jacob Druckman, Earle Brown, Roger Reynolds, and Bernard Rands. During this time, he also collaborated with jazz arranger Gil Evans in New York, and pursued further studies with composer György Ligeti in Hamburg, Germany (1982-84). After teaching music composition from 1986-90 at the Oberlin Conservatory of Music, Daugherty joined the School of Music at the University of Michigan (Ann Arbor) in 1991, where he is Professor of Composition and a mentor to many of today's most talented young composers.

Daugherty has been Composer-in-Residence with the Louisville Symphony Orchestra (2000), Detroit Symphony Orchestra (1999-2003), Colorado Symphony Orchestra (2001-02), Cabrillo Festival of Contemporary Music (2001-04, 2006-08, 2011), Westshore Symphony Orchestra (2005-06), Eugene Symphony (2006), Henry Mancini Summer Institute (2006), Music from Angel Fire Chamber Music Festival (2006), Pacific Symphony (2010-11), Chattanooga Symphony (2012-13), New Century Chamber Orchestra (2013), and Albany Symphony (2015).

Daugherty has received numerous awards, distinctions, and fellowships for his music, including: a Fulbright Fellowship (1977), the Kennedy Center Friedheim Award (1989), the Goddard Lieberson Fellowship from the American Academy of Arts and Letters (1991), fellowships from the National Endowment for the Arts (1992) and the Guggenheim Foundation (1996), and the Stoeger Prize from the Chamber Music Society of Lincoln Center (2000). In 2005, Daugherty received the Lancaster Symphony Orchestra Composer's Award, and in 2007, the Delaware Symphony Orchestra selected Daugherty as the winner of the A.I. DuPont Award. Also in 2007, he received the American Bandmasters Association Ostwald Award for his composition *Raise the Roof* for Timpani and Symphonic Band. Daugherty has been named "Outstanding Classical Composer" at the Detroit Music Awards in 2007, 2009 and 2010. His GRAMMY® award winning recordings can be heard on Albany, Argo, Delos, Equilibrium, Klavier, Naxos and Nonesuch labels.

Paul Robeson in Eugene O'Neill's *The Emperor Jones* (1933)

COMPOSER'S NOTE

Strut (1989) for string orchestra was commissioned by the New York State School Music Association and first performed by the New York All-State String Orchestra, conducted by Larry Rachleff, at the 1989 NYSSMA Conference on October 15, 1989.

The buoyancy and fearless fiddling of *Strut* for string orchestra reflects the visionary optimism of the Harlem Renaissance. From 1920-1930, the Harlem Renaissance marked an unprecedented outburst of creative activity in all fields of African-American art, literature and music. Actor, singer and political activist Paul Robeson (1898-1976) was a central figure of this new and exciting form of urban cultural expression. Imagining a youthful and optimistic Robeson strutting down 125th street during the Harlem Renaissance, I have created vibrant musical motives, themes and syncopations, which are woven into a lively rhythmic tapestry.

—Michael Daugherty

INSTRUMENTATION

String Orchestra:

Violin I
Violin II
Viola
Violoncello
Contrabass

Duration: *ca.* 6 minutes

STRUT
for String Orchestra

Michael Daugherty
(1989)

979-0-051-09682-4

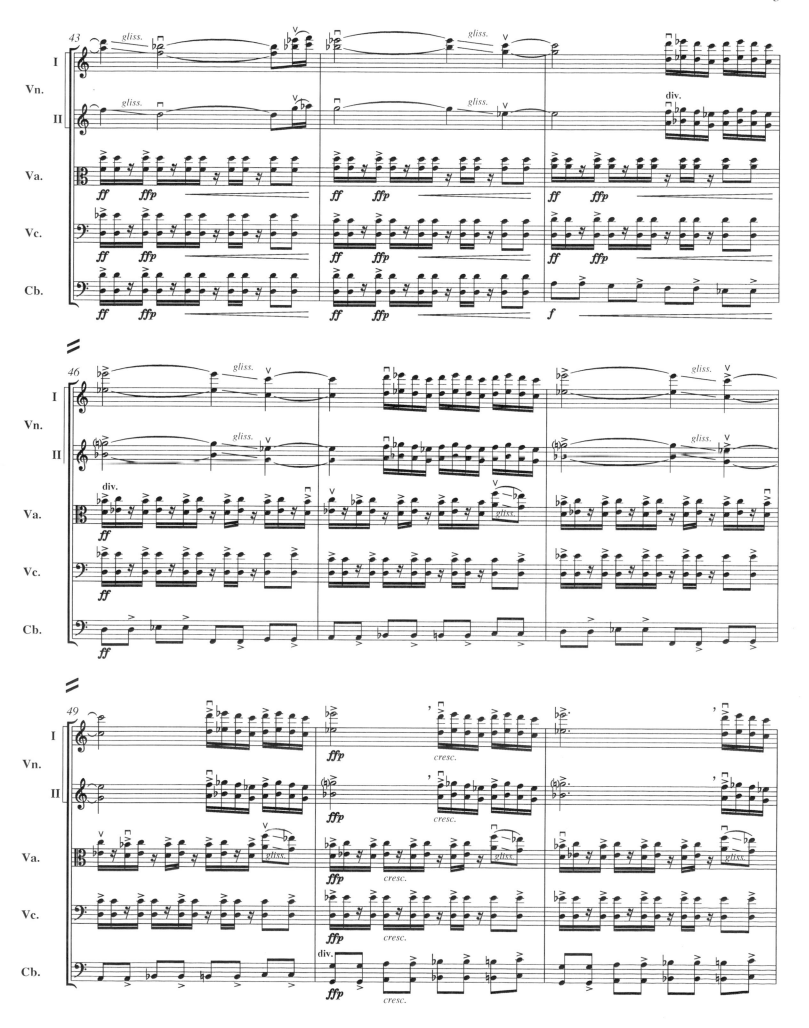

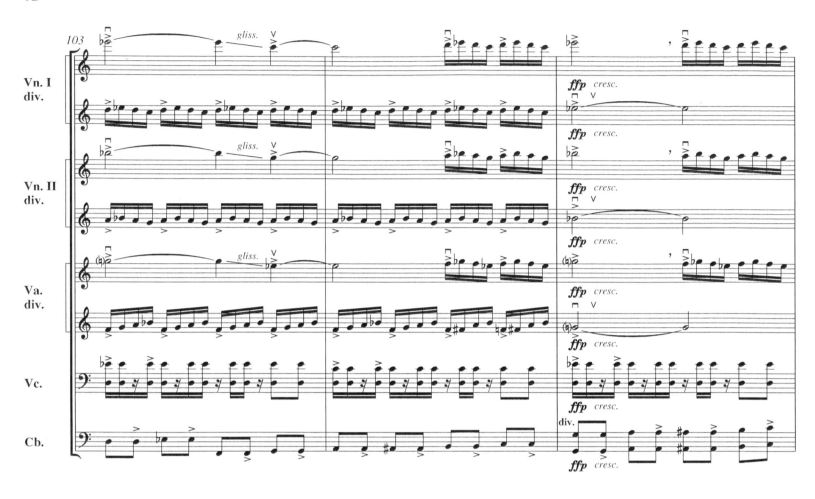

I **Pressing Forward**

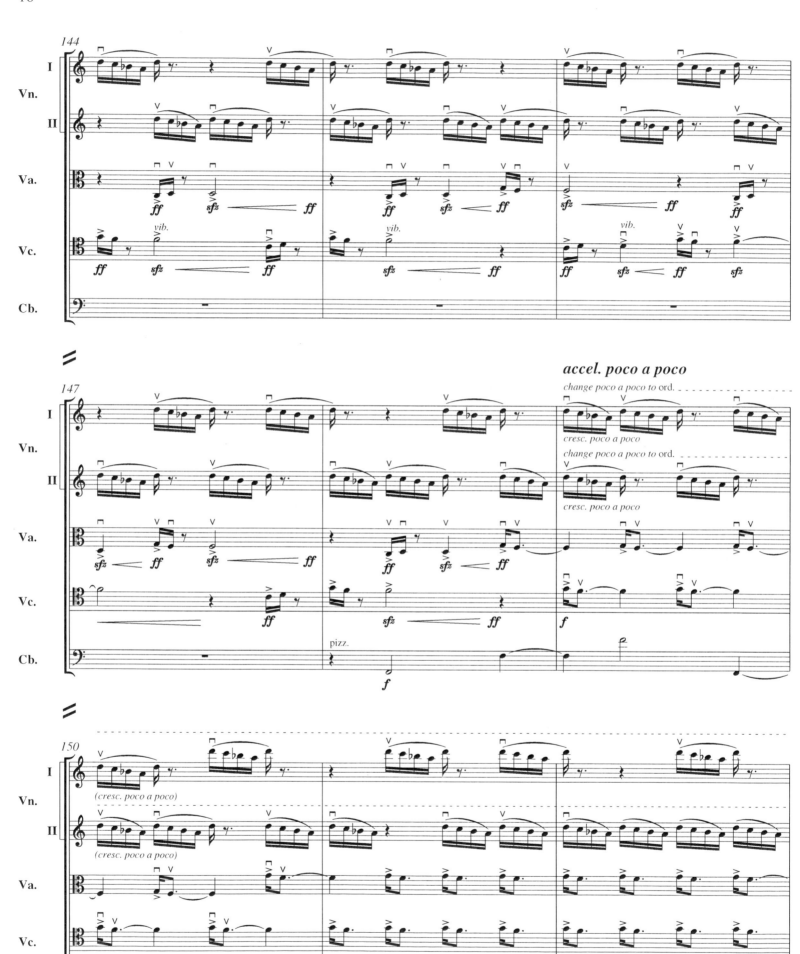

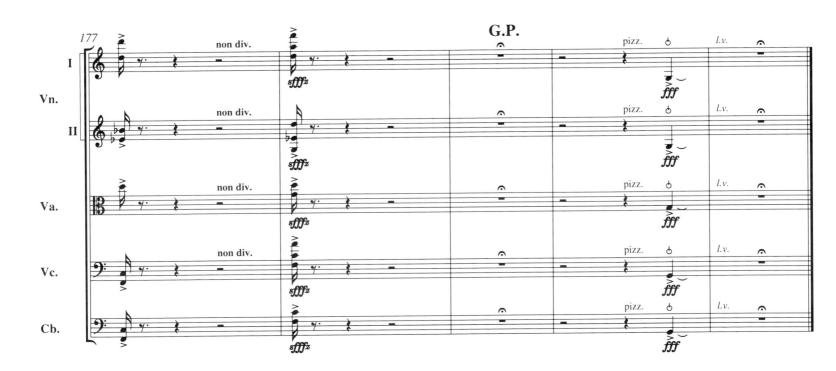